KAMALA HARRIS

KAMALA HARRIS

Madam Vice President

Heather E. Schwartz

LERNER PUBLICATIONS ◆ MINNEAPOLIS

Lerner Publications Company
An imprint of Lerner Publishing Group, Inc.
241 First Avenue North
Minneapolis, MN 55401 USA

For reading levels and more information, look up this title at www.lernerbooks.com.

Image credits: AP Photo/Carolyn Kaster, pp. 2, 8, 23; Office of Senator Kamala Harris, p. 6; Rowland Scherman/U.S. National Archives and Records Administration, p. 9; AP Photo/ Meg Kinnard, p. 10; David Monack/Wikimedia Commons, p. 12; AP Photo/Anne Chadwick Williams, p. 16; AP Photo/George Nikitin, p. 17; AP Photo/Faye Sadou, p. 18; AP Photo/Damian Dovarganes, p. 19; AP Photo/Jeff Chiu, pp. 20, 24; Andy Dean Photography/Shutterstock.com, p. 21; LaMarr McDaniel/Shutterstock.com, p. 22; AP Photo/Tony Avelar, p. 25; AP Photo/Eric Risberg, p. 27; AP Photo/Anthony Behar/Sipa USA, p. 28; AP Photo/J. Scott Applewhite, p. 29; Sheila Fitzgerald/Shutterstock.com, p. 30; AP Photo/Willy Sanjuan, p. 32; Sundry Photography/ Shutterstock.com, p. 33; Maverick Pictures/Shutterstock.com, p. 34; AP Photo/David J. Phillip, p. 35; AP Photo/Rod Lamkey Jr., p. 36; Thomas J. O'Halloran/Library of Congress, p. 37; AP Photo/Andrew Harnik, p. 38. Cover: AP Photo/Carolyn Kaster.

Main body text set in Rotis Serif Std 55 Regular. Typeface provided by Adobe Systems.

Editor: Rebecca Higgins **Designer:** Lauren Cooper **Photo Editor:** Brianna Kaiser

Library of Congress Cataloging-in-Publication Data

Names: Schwartz, Heather E., author.
Title: Kamala Harris : Madam Vice President / Heather E. Schwartz.
Description: Minneapolis : Lerner Publications, [2021] | Series: Gateway biographies | Includes bibliographical references and index. | Audience: Ages 9–14 | Audience: Grades 4–6 | Summary: "Senator Kamala Harris is known as a tough prosecutor. She made history as the first Black and Indian woman to lead a major ticket. Follow her fight to the White House!"— Provided by publisher.
Identifiers: LCCN 2020046119 (print) | LCCN 2020046120 (ebook) | ISBN 9781728427829 (library binding) | ISBN 9781728427836 (ebook)
Subjects: LCSH: Harris, Kamala, 1964–-Juvenile literature. | Women legislators—United States— Biography—Juvenile literature. | Legislators—United States—Biography—Juvenile literature. | Women presidential candidates—United States—Biography—Juvenile literature. | Presidential candidates—United States—Biography—Juvenile literature. | United States. Congress. Senate— Biography—Juvenile literature.
Classification: LCC E901.1.H37 S39 2021 (print) | LCC E901.1.H37 (ebook) | DDC 328.73092 [B]—dc23

LC record available at https://lccn.loc.gov/2020046119
LC ebook record available at https://lccn.loc.gov/2020046120

Manufactured in the United States of America
1-49344-49450-10/29/2020

TABLE OF CONTENTS

US senator Kamala Harris of California had already made history many times throughout her career. On August 19, 2020, she prepared to take the stage at the Democratic National Convention and shatter even more barriers. A week earlier, she'd been selected by Democratic presidential candidate Joe Biden as his running mate.

Normally, cheering crowds filled the convention, but the COVID-19 pandemic forced the event online. Before Harris addressed the viewers from the Chase Center in Wilmington, Delaware, a video featuring her sister, stepdaughter, and niece introduced her as a role model, a friend, and a rock of stability for a large blended family. When Harris stepped up to the podium, the unusual circumstances didn't take away from her commitment and conviction as she accepted the nomination. She was the first Black woman and the first Asian woman to become a vice-presidential nominee.

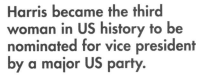

Harris became the third woman in US history to be nominated for vice president by a major US party.

Harris spoke about problems facing the country, including racism, inequities in education and health care, and the pandemic. She talked about her family, including her mother, who'd raised her for a life of public service. She urged voters to elect Joe Biden for a better America. And she acknowledged her place in history and how far the country had come since its founding.

"That I am here tonight is a testament to the dedication of generations before me," Harris said. "Women and men who believed so fiercely in the promise of equality, liberty, and justice for all. We're not often taught their stories. But as Americans, we all stand on their shoulders."

Growing Up

Kamala Devi Harris was born on October 20, 1964, in Oakland, California. Her father, Donald Harris, immigrated to the United States from Jamaica and taught economics at Stanford University. Her mother, Shyamala Gopalan, came from India and worked as a cancer researcher. Harris and Gopalan met at the University of California, Berkeley, and both believed in the civil rights movement. In the 1950s and 1960s the civil rights movement fought for fair treatment for Black Americans. After marrying and having Kamala, they gave her an early start in politics. They brought her to protests in her stroller. As a family, they stood up against racism and fought for equal rights.

Martin Luther King Jr. (*center*) was one of the leaders of the civil rights movement.

When Kamala was three, her family grew. Her younger sister, Maya, was born in 1967. Four years later, their parents divorced. Kamala and Maya lived with their mother, a strong role model, in Berkeley. She taught her daughters to solve their own problems and always do their best.

As a young student, Kamala had another brush with politics. She was part of the busing program to increase desegregation of schools. Racist policies prevented people of color from living in certain neighborhoods. So to desegregate schools more, politicians decided to bus some kids to different schools.

Kamala and Maya grew up connecting with their culture from both sides of the family. On weekends they attended a Black Baptist church as well as a Hindu temple. They also took trips with their parents to Jamaica and India.

When Kamala was twelve, she, her mother, and her sister moved to Canada. Gopalan accepted a job in Montreal, Quebec. She would teach at McGill University and research cancer at Jewish General Hospital.

Kamala attends church in 2019.

Kamala wasn't excited about this change. "The thought of moving away from sunny California in February, in the middle of the school year, to a French-speaking foreign city covered in twelve feet [4 m] of snow was distressing, to say the least," she recalls.

What's in a Name?

Kamala means "lotus." It's also a name for the Hindu goddess Lakshmi. Kamala's mother chose the name because it represented their Indian culture and a reverence for strong women.

But Kamala and Maya still had a connection to California. They spent summers there with their father in Palo Alto. During the school year, they lived in Montreal with their mother.

The first school Kamala attended in Montreal was for French-speaking students. Gopalan knew that immersing Kamala in the language would help her learn it faster. Later, Kamala went to a fine arts middle school and took up violin, French horn, and kettle drum. Around then, she organized her first protest with Maya. Their apartment building had a policy that forbade kids from playing on the front lawn. They didn't think it was fair. By protesting, they won the right to play there.

After middle school, Kamala attended Westmount High School for English-speaking students. She was a member of the pep club and part of a small dance troupe, Midnight Magic. The group performed at senior centers and community centers. During her last year of high school, she helped organize a group of girls to attend a big senior dance together so that no one would feel left out if they didn't have a date.

Kamala's dream was to become a lawyer. She attended Howard University in Washington, DC, a historically Black college and former US Supreme Court justice Thurgood Marshall's alma mater. It felt like the right place to start her career.

A Historic Win

At Howard University, Harris studied political science and economics with the children of civil rights movement leaders Jesse Jackson and Andrew Young. She embraced the opportunity to connect with her Black identity at

Harris holds a special place in her heart for her alma mater, Howard University.

college. She met other students there who, like her, had one Black parent and one parent from another culture.

Harris developed her political identity at Howard University. She was recruited for and joined the debate team. She also protested against apartheid, a social system in South Africa that didn't give Black people the same political and economic rights as white people. Harris even ran her first political campaign, winning and becoming the freshman representative of the Liberal Arts Student Council. She joined the oldest Black sorority in the US too—Alpha Kappa Alpha.

After graduating from Howard in 1986, Harris went to the University of California, Hastings College of the Law, in San Francisco. She was president of the Black Law Students Association. She also worked with the Legal Education Opportunity Program to create more opportunities for students of color.

Harris graduated in 1989. She passed the bar exam and began a job as deputy district attorney with the Alameda County District Attorney's Office. Her family was not excited to see her become a prosecutor. They associated the job with people who used their power to oppress Black people. Harris had other ideas. She felt she could change the system by fighting it from the inside.

Her specialty as deputy district attorney was prosecuting criminals accused of crimes against children. She also worked on murder and robbery cases, including gang violence and drug trafficking. She began to get a reputation for being tough on criminals.

In 1998 Harris became managing attorney of the Career Criminal Unit of the San Francisco District Attorney's Office. She prosecuted criminals who were considered serial offenders. Next, she became the head of the San Francisco City Attorney's Division on Families and Children and focused on helping underprivileged people.

Harris was frustrated working under San Francisco district attorney Terence Hallinan, and in 2002, she decided to run against the Republican. "I believed the district attorney was undercutting the whole idea of what a progressive prosecutor could be," Harris said. "My vision of a progressive prosecutor was someone who used the power of the office with a sense of fairness, perspective, and experience, someone who was clear about the need to hold serious criminals accountable and who understood that the best way to create safe communities was to prevent crime in the first place. To do those things effectively, you also need to run a professional operation."

Harris's family and friends helped her grassroots campaign. Gopalan filled envelopes to send to voters. The mailers let people know that Harris was against the death penalty and favored treatment programs instead of jail for first-time, nonviolent offenders. When Harris met voters face-to-face, she often stood behind an ironing board she used as a table. She also had posters and duct tape.

She learned to be comfortable talking about herself with voters. She set up in front of grocery stores, knocked on doors, and waited at bus stops.

At first, her chances didn't look good. But as people got to know Harris, they liked her policies and believed she'd fight for them. In 2003 she beat Hallinan with 56.5 percent of the votes. Her predecessor left his office in a state of disrepair, and she got to work right away. She repainted it, replaced the broken copy machine, and introduced a fresh attitude as the new boss.

"If staffers tried to leave in the evening before Harris thought they should, she shouted, 'Well, I guess justice has been done! Everybody's going home,'" recounted one reporter.

Harris's commitment to the people of San Francisco was clear. She led one of the biggest legal departments in the nation as its first Black, first Asian, and first woman district attorney.

Difficult Decisions

When Harris took office in 2004, the people of San Francisco got what they wanted—a strong-minded district attorney who was determined to fight crime. She was dedicated to those she served. But some of her decisions were controversial. Shortly after she took office, a young police officer in the city was shot and killed while conducting an investigation. The officer's family, the police union, and some politicians felt Harris should seek the death penalty for the suspect. But Harris stuck to her principles and aimed for life in prison instead. The killer was found guilty and sentenced to life without parole.

Sisterly Support

Harris's sister, Maya Harris, is a friend and a huge supporter. Like Harris, she credits their mother for raising them to be leaders.

Maya Harris also went into public service. She worked at the American Civil Liberties Union and the Ford Foundation, and served on Hillary Clinton's 2016 presidential campaign. She also was one of the youngest law school deans in the US at Lincoln Law School in San Jose, California.

She was working as a political analyst for MSNBC when she decided to leave the job to run her sister's presidential campaign.

Maya (*center*) inaugurated Harris (*right*) as attorney general in 2011.

Harris takes the oath of office in 2004 with her mother at her side.

During her first years in office, the criminal conviction rate in San Francisco rose due to drug prosecutions. Some people thought there shouldn't be an increase, while police pressured Harris to try more cases. But Harris once again relied on her morals and only brought cases she thought should be tried. She also helped those who were prosecuted. In 2005 she started Back on Track to help young, first-time drug offenders reenter society after serving their time. The program helped about three hundred people get their high school degrees and find jobs.

Harris wrote a children's book, *Superheroes Are Everywhere.*

Around 2008 Harris made a controversial decision to treat truancy as a crime. Parents who regularly did not send their kids to school could be held accountable by her office. They could be fined or arrested. The move was more about making sure kids got their education—which could lead to better jobs in the future—than punishing parents. The truancy rates fell. But not everyone agreed it helped more than it hurt.

On November 12, 2008, Harris announced that she would run for attorney general of California in the 2010 election. A year after the announcement, she published *Smart on Crime: A Career Prosecutor's Plan to Make Us Safer,* a book that laid out her ideas for preventing crime and stopping convicted criminals from committing more crimes.

"Public health practitioners know that the most beneficial use of resources is to prevent an outbreak, not treat it," she wrote. "Instead of just reacting to a crime every time it is committed, we have to step back and figure out how to disrupt the routes of infection."

In June 2010, she was nominated as the Democratic candidate in a tight race against Attorney General Steve Cooley. On November 2, 2010, election night, it looked as though Cooley had won. By about eleven at night, he was so confident he gave a speech to his supporters declaring his victory.

But as the vote count continued the next day, Harris took the lead by about twenty-two thousand votes. Harris was determined the winner by about fifty thousand votes three weeks later. On June 8, 2010, she gave her primary victory speech, emphasizing the core values of democracy.

Harris gives her first news conference after winning the attorney general race.

"[It] is about recognizing the needs of poor people," she said. "It is about recognizing the needs of people who have been the subject of hate or bias. It is about protecting all vulnerable people. We will be tough and smart to get that job done."

When Harris was sworn in on January 3, 2011, she became California's first Black, first Asian, and first female attorney general. She'd always considered it her job to stand by the words "For the People." She planned to stand up for the people she served in her new role.

Harris meets with District Attorney Bonnie Dumanis of San Diego in 2010.

Rising Star

Harris quickly established herself as an attorney general who wouldn't back down under pressure. One of the first issues she dealt with involved settlement money for homeowners who were unable to pay their mortgages. Banks had given them loans they couldn't afford, and they were losing their homes. Banks offered California a $2 billion settlement. Other attorneys general were ready to accept the offer. But it wasn't enough to help all the Californians who needed relief, and Harris refused it.

Over 235,000 Californians lost their homes to foreclosure in 2008.

When she took a stand for her state's homeowners, she had little support. Many other politicians, including President Barack Obama, wanted her to accept the money and move forward.

Harris respected the Obama administration, but she sympathized with homeowners. She could remember how much it meant to her family when her mother bought their first home. She held out, believing she could get more money for the people of her state. In 2012 her persistence finally paid off. The banks offered California

$20 billion. Help was on its way for homeowners, and Harris proved she would stand up for the people who counted on her.

Harris's stand captured the nation's attention. The media portrayed her as a rising star in politics. Some speculated she might run to become a US senator or the governor of California. Some even thought she might run for president in 2016. Her next move wasn't to a new job, but it took her to the national stage.

An Ally and a Friend

Attorneys general in some states supported Harris's decision to continue fighting the banks for homeowners. One of them was Beau Biden, Delaware's attorney general, who had decided to do the same. During the tense negotiations, they developed a close friendship. They talked about feeling uncomfortable opposing Obama and their experiences growing up with successful parents. Harris first knew Joe Biden as her friend Beau Biden's father.

Beau Biden delivers a 2012 speech in support of Obama's reelection.

Though they sometimes disagree, Harris and Obama have always respected each other.

In September 2012, Harris was invited to speak at the Democratic National Convention. She would have six minutes at the high-profile event supporting Obama's run for a second term. She talked about the housing crisis and how Obama handled it. Though they disagreed about how much to push the banks, they were both fighting for the American people.

"Millions of Americans know that feeling of walking through the front door of their own home for the first time—the feeling of reaching for opportunity and finding it," Harris said. "That's the choice in this election. It's a choice between an America where opportunity is open to everyone, where everyone plays by the same set of rules, or a philosophy that tilts the playing field to help the wealthiest few."

Her appearance at the Democratic National Convention raised her profile even more. But Harris was happy as attorney general and not nearly finished with her term. She continued her work, gaining attention again in 2013 for taking a stand against California state law. When the California Supreme Court ruled marriage was between a man and a woman, Harris refused to support the ruling. She knew that people's rights shouldn't be limited by their sexuality. When the ruling was overturned, it opened the door for marriage equality.

In 2013 Harris met Douglas Emhoff, an entertainment attorney, on a blind date, and they immediately hit it off. In August 2014, they married in a ceremony presided

Harris officiates a wedding ceremony for a same-sex couple in 2013.

Douglas, Ella, and Cole Emhoff stand together during a campaign event for Harris.

over by her sister, Maya. Harris became a stepmother to Emhoff's two children, Cole and Ella. They became a blended family with Cole and Ella calling Harris Momala.

In November, Harris was reelected as California's attorney general. She won 55 percent of the votes and was set to serve another four-year term. She quickly took steps to improve law enforcement training. The first of its kind in the US, the training was meant to make sure people in the community were treated fairly by law enforcement.

In September 2015, Harris launched OpenJustice. It tracked data on crime and the criminal justice system, making it easier to see where improvements could be made. The initiative also made law enforcement's work more transparent and built trust with the community.

Winning a Senate Seat

By January 13, 2015, Harris was ready for a new challenge. She announced she would run for the US Senate. With her eye on the 2016 election, she started fundraising and focusing on her campaign. From the beginning, she promised to fight for Californians—especially middle-class families, children, students, immigrants, and senior citizens. Harris had a promising campaign. The Democratic Party endorsed her in February 2016. She also had the support of Obama and Biden.

Harris used her campaign to speak out for immigration and criminal-justice reform. She wanted to increase the minimum wage and protect women's reproductive rights. Harris had no trouble beating her opponent, fellow Democrat Loretta Sanchez.

When Harris was elected in November 2016, she became the second Black woman and the first South Asian American

A Senator's Job

Each state in the US is represented by two senators. They are elected to six-year terms. Senators vote on new laws. They also approve presidential appointments to the Supreme Court and other offices, ratify treaties with foreign countries, try impeachment cases, and even select a vice president in some situations.

senator in US history. In her victory speech, she echoed her intention to fight for principles that would help Californians and all Americans.

"Our ideals are at stake right now and we all have to fight for who we are," she said "I believe it's a pivotal moment in the history of our country. We are a great country. And part of what makes us great is fighting for our ideals."

Harris took office in January 2017. On the night she won her Senate seat, Republican candidate Donald Trump was elected president of the United States. Harris strongly opposed his politics and, like many Democrats, was upset that he had won. She'd heard his controversial comments about immigrants and women.

Harris applauds her staff's hard work during her inauguration.

In January 2017, Trump became president of the US.

Harris addressed her campaign staff with the message that though the Senate race was over, they would have to continue their work and their fight. "It's gonna be a campaign to fight for everything that motivated us to run for this office in the first place," she said. "Because I think there is no question that everything that we have been talking about in terms of everything from criminal justice reform to climate change to immigration . . . is now really on the line."

Harris began speaking out against Trump's new policies and picks for political offices. She opposed his executive order to ban Syrian refugees and limit refugees from other countries with large populations of Muslims. Harris said it was a racist policy that discriminated against refugees for their religion. In February she introduced a Senate bill that would guarantee legal help to refugees blocked from entering the US.

That month Harris said she'd voted against Betsy DeVos, noting Trump's choice for US secretary of education was not experienced or curious about education. Harris also voted against Senator Jeff Sessions, Trump's pick for US attorney general, pointing out his history of opposing civil rights. After Sessions took office, Harris called on him to resign when reports came out that he'd lied about

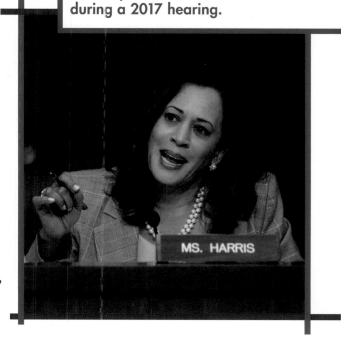

Harris questions Sessions during a 2017 hearing.

MS. HARRIS

his communications with the Russian government. And in April, Harris opposed Judge Neil Gorsuch, Trump's nominee for the US Supreme Court, based on his record of favoring corporations over workers.

That month Harris visited the Middle East and met with US troops from California and people living in a Syrian refugee camp. Hearing firsthand about the horrors they'd faced strengthened her resolve to create US policies that would help them.

"I will continue to support our brave men and women as they work . . . and defend the security interests of the United States," she said. "It is critical we have a sound,

Harris is known for standing up to the Trump administration.

detailed, and long-term national security strategy to combat terrorism in the Middle East, and an immigration policy that provides a safe haven to those fleeing violence and oppression."

In June 2017, Harris drew on all the skills she'd learned in court as a prosecutor. She played a key role at a Senate Select Committee on Intelligence hearing about possible ties between Russia and Trump's presidential campaign.

During the hearing, she aggressively questioned Deputy Attorney General Rod Rosenstein. Harris interrupted Rosenstein to point out that he wasn't answering yes or no to direct questions. The committee chair, Senator Richard Burr, stopped her, calling on her to be courteous. But many believed Harris had been silenced unfairly. Other senators, including fellow Democrat Elizabeth Warren, supported Harris and her approach to uncover the truth.

At that hearing, Harris questioned Attorney General Sessions about conversations he'd had with Trump. When he wouldn't answer directly, she kept asking until he said he was nervous. Burr stopped her again.

Harris proved she wasn't afraid to ask important questions. She gained attention as a powerful politician who wouldn't back down under pressure.

Presidential Contender

Harris continued questioning people in power and government policies. She was on the Senate Homeland Security and Governmental Affairs Committee, the Senate Select Committee on Intelligence, and the Senate Committee on the Budget. In January 2018, she was appointed to the US Senate Judiciary Committee. It dealt with such issues as criminal justice reform, federal criminal law, human rights, immigration law, consumer protection, and internet privacy.

"I look forward to the chance to continue to provide a voice for our most vulnerable communities, work on issues I've handled since my earliest days in the Alameda County District Attorney's office, and defend California in the face of this Administration's repeated attacks on our values," she said.

In April, Harris questioned Facebook CEO Mark Zuckerberg during a Senate hearing. He was there to talk about his decision to hide a data leak of personal information from eighty-seven million users. The data had allowed Russia to target ads for Trump during the presidential campaign. Harris's questions grew more pointed as Zuckerberg failed to answer directly. The following month, she questioned Homeland Security secretary Kirstjen Nielsen about the Trump administration's policy to separate immigrant families entering the US illegally. Harris was strongly opposed to the policy, which took children from their families and didn't provide tracking so they could eventually be reunited.

Harris speaks at an event protesting Trump's decision to break up migrant families.

In June 2018, Harris visited Otay Mesa Detention Center in San Diego, California, and met with migrant mothers who had been separated from their children. By then Trump had signed an executive order to end the separations, but it was too late to help families already split apart. Harris reported on the women's grief and called for Trump to reunite separated families. She also called for Nielsen's resignation.

Harris had a busy January 2019. She published her memoir, *The Truths We Hold: An American Journey.* Then, on Martin Luther King Jr. Day, she made a big announcement. She said she would run for president of the United States. She showed her dedication to help others with the slogan Kamala Harris for the People. On January 27, 2019, she officially launched her campaign with a speech about the Trump administration's failures

Supporters hold signs and cheer for Harris at a campaign rally.

Harris campaigns at a college in New Hampshire.

and why she decided to run.

"We are here because the American Dream and our American democracy are under attack and on the line like never before," she said. "We are here at this moment in time because we must answer a fundamental question. Who are we? Who are we as Americans? So, let's answer that question to the world and each other right here and right now. America: we are better than this."

If nominated by the Democratic Party, Harris had the chance to become America's first female, Black, Asian American president. Winning the nomination would be tough with so many contenders, including Warren, former Indiana mayor Pete Buttigieg, Senator Bernie Sanders, and Joe Biden. But Harris held her own as she continued her campaign and earned the spotlight during an August Democratic debate.

Harris (*fourth from right*) stands alongside other candidates hoping to became the Democratic Party's nominee for president in a 2019 debate.

At the debate, Harris criticized Biden's past work with segregationists. And she called him out for opposing legislation early in his career that enforced the busing system that had helped integrate schools. "There was a little girl in California who was part of the second class to integrate her public schools and she was bused to school every day," she told Biden. "And that little girl was me."

Harris campaigned most of the year while continuing to work as a senator. But it became clear that she wouldn't win the nomination. In December she ended her campaign. But she said she was still committed to fighting for justice for everyone in America.

Vice-Presidential Pick

Harris started 2020 speaking out at Trump's impeachment trial. Trump had withheld aid from Ukraine while asking that country's president to investigate Trump's political rival, Biden, and his son Hunter Biden. Harris called for justice and voted to convict Trump on charges of obstructing Congress and abusing his power. While Trump was acquitted in February, the country was on the brink of several events set to rock the nation.

The pandemic and soon another story showed racial disparities in the US. A Black man in Minneapolis, Minnesota, named George Floyd died after a white police officer held his knee to Floyd's neck for more than seven minutes. Protesters demanded justice. Some

Harris speaks at a press conference before Trump's impeachment trial.

criticized Harris for her record of being tough on crime as attorney general of California. They claimed she was on the side of the police officers. But Harris spoke out against systemic racism in the US and called for police reforms.

Meanwhile, Biden had become the Democratic front-runner in the presidential race. And he was mulling over who to choose as a running mate.

By late summer, several contenders for the spot had emerged. Harris was one of them, along with former national security adviser Susan Rice, Michigan governor Gretchen Whitmer, and Warren, among others. In August, Biden chose Harris and called her a "fearless fighter for the little guy" and "one of the country's finest public servants."

Harris's Hero

Harris is inspired by the late representative Shirley Chisholm, a fellow Democrat. In 1968 Chisholm became the first Black woman in Congress. A few years later, in 1972, she ran for president. She became the first Black woman to aim for a major political party's presidential nomination. Though she did not win the nomination, she continued serving in government until 1983.

As Biden's vice-presidential pick, Harris became the first Black woman and first Indian American woman nominated for a national office by a major party. Everyone was talking about Harris and her new role. Trump tweeted that she was wrong for the country. Obama, Hillary Clinton, Sanders, and others tweeted their support. Her family proudly chimed in with congratulations on social media too.

With the election less than three months away, Harris accepted the nomination at the Democratic National Convention. She joined Biden's campaign and continued to speak out on problems facing the nation.

Harris and Biden join hands after the 2020 Democratic National Convention.

Harris Helping Moms

Harris knew that Black women in the US died at a higher-than-average rate during pregnancy. In 2018 and 2019, she worked on the Maternal CARE Act, which would put money toward solving the problem. Its goals were to end racial bias in medicine and provide equal access to quality health care for Black women. In 2020 Harris worked to pass the Black Maternal Health Momnibus Act. It focused on specific groups including mothers who are veterans and mothers in prison.

Nearly 160 million Americans voted to decide the next president and vice president. It took several days to count the mail-in ballots, which were plentiful since many chose to vote by mail due to COVID-19. Election day came and went without an answer.

Finally, on November 7, 2020, the media declared Biden and Harris the winners. That evening, Harris addressed the nation. She promised to be a vice president for all Americans. She vowed to focus her attention on the pandemic, economy, racial justice, and climate change. "The road ahead will not be easy. But America is ready," she said. "And so are Joe and I."

IMPORTANT DATES

1964 Kamala Devi Harris is born on October 20.

1986 She graduates from Howard University.

1989 Harris graduates from the University of California, Hastings College of the Law.

She becomes deputy district attorney with the Alameda County District Attorney's Office.

1998 Harris becomes managing attorney of the Career Criminal Unit of the San Francisco District Attorney's Office.

2003 Harris is elected San Francisco's first African American, first Asian, and first woman district attorney.

2009 She publishes *Smart on Crime: A Career Prosecutor's Plan to Make Us Safer.*

2010 Harris is elected California's first Black, first Asian, and first woman attorney general.

2012 She speaks at the Democratic National Convention.

2014 She marries Douglas Emhoff and becomes stepmom to his children.

2016 Harris is elected to the US Senate. She is the second Black woman and first South Asian American US senator.

2019 Harris publishes *The Truths We Hold: An American Journey.*

She launches a campaign for president of the United States in January.

She exits the presidential race in December.

2020 Biden chooses Harris as his running mate, and she accepts the nomination for vice president of the United States.

Biden and Harris win the presidential election.

SOURCE NOTES

8   "Transcript: Kamala Harris' DNC Speech," CNN, August 20, 2020, https://www.cnn.com/2020/08/19/politics/kamala-harris-speech-transcript/index.html.

11 Casey Tolan, "Why Some of Kamala Harris' Biggest Fans Are in Canada," *San Jose (CA) Mercury News*, last modified May 8, 2019, https://www.mercurynews.com/2019/05/07/kamala-harris-high-school-montreal-canada-yearbook/.

14 David Siders, " 'Ruthless': How Kamala Harris Won Her First Race," *Politico Magazine*, January 24, 2017, https://www.politico.com/magazine/story/2019/01/24/kamala-harris-2020-history-224126.

15 Elizabeth Weil, "Kamala Harris Takes Her Shot," *Atlantic*, May 2019, https://www.theatlantic.com/magazine/archive/2019/05/kamala-harris-2020-campaign/586033/.

18 Ben Christopher, "What California Knows about Kamala Harris," ABC 10, August 11, 2020, https://www.abc10.com/article/news/local/california/california-kamala-harris/103-da247ba2-1ac8-43d0-896b-99b1f016e69e.

20 "Kamala Harris Attorney General Victory Speech in San Francisco—2010 California Primary," YouTube video, 15:51, posted by Zennie62 YouTube Oakland News Now Commentary Vlog, June 9, 2010, https://www.youtube.com/watch?v =4U6MaWWzin4.

23 "Kamala Harris DNC Speech," *Politico*, September 5, 2012, https://www.politico.com/story/2012/09/kamala-harris-dnc -speech-text-080799.

27 "See California Senator-Elect Kamala Harris' Victory Speech," NBC News, November 9, 2016, https://www.nbcnews.com /video/see-california-senator-elect-kamala-harris-victory -speech-804549699735.

28 Marina Pitofsky, "Harris Shares Video Addressing Staffers the Night Trump Was Elected," Hill, November 9, 2016, https:// thehill.com/homenews/campaign/469760-harris-shares-video -addressing-staffers-the-night-trump-was-elected-this-is.

29–30 "Senator Harris Returns from Trip to the Middle East," Kamala D. Harris, US Senator for California, April 17, 2017, https://www.harris.senate.gov/news/press-releases/senator-harris-returns-from-trip-to-the-middle-east.

31 "Senator Harris Joins Senate Judiciary Committee," Kamala D. Harris, US Senator for California, January 9, 2018, https://www.harris.senate.gov/news/press-releases/senator-harris-joins-senate-judiciary-committee.

34 Maeve Reston, "Kamala Harris Officially Launches 2020 Presidential Campaign," CNN, January 28, 2019, https://www.cnn.com/2019/01/27/politics/kamala-harris-2020-presidential-campaign/index.html.

35 P. R. Lockhart, "Joe Biden's Record on School Desegregation Busing, Explained," Vox, July 16, 2019, https://www.vox.com/policy-and-politics/2019/6/28/18965923/joe-biden-school-desegregation-busing-democratic-primary.

37 Christopher Cadelago and Caitlin Oprysko, "Biden Picks Kamala as VP Nominee," *Politico*, August 11, 2020, https://www.politico.com/news/2020/08/11/joe-biden-vp-pick-kamala-harris-393768.

39 Prakash, Neha, "Read the Full Transcript of Kamala Harris's Speech as Vice-President Elect," Yahoo! Finance, November 7, 2020, https://ca.finance.yahoo.com/news/read-full-transcript-kamala-harriss-022600804.html.

SELECTED BIBLIOGRAPHY

Betancourt, Bianca. "Kamala Harris' Family Reacts to Her History-Making Vice President Nomination." *Harper's Bazaar*, August 12, 2020. https://www.harpersbazaar.com/culture/politics/a33584178 /kamala-harris-family-reacts-to-vice-president-nomination/.

Breuninger, Kevin. "Kamala Harris Attacks Biden's Record on Busing and Working with Segregationists in Vicious Exchange at Democratic Debate." CNBC. Last modified June 2, 2019. https://www.cnbc .com/2019/06/27/harris-attacks-bidens-record-on-busing-and -working-with-segregationists.html.

"California State Attorney General Kamala Harris at the 2012 Democratic National Convention." YouTube video, 6:05. Posted by the 2020 Democratic National Convention, September 6, 2012. https://www .youtube.com/watch?v=SKXNd5sRJDw.

Hubbard, Lauren, "Who Is Kamala Harris' Husband, Douglas Emhoff?" *Town & Country*, August 11, 2020. https://www.townandcountrymag .com/society/politics/a27256864/kamala-harris-husband-douglas -emhoff-facts/.

McNamee, Gregory Lewis. "Kamala Harris, United States Senator." *Encyclopaedia Britannica*, August 12, 2020. https://www.britannica .com/biography/Kamala-Harris.

"See California Senator-Elect Kamala Harris' Victory Speech." NBC News, November 9, 2016. https://www.nbcnews.com/video/see-california -senator-elect-kamala-harris-victory-speech-804549699735.

Summers, Juana. "Howard University Shaped Kamala Harris' Path to Political Heights." NPR, August 19, 2020. https://www.npr .org/2020/08/19/903716274/howard-university-shaped-kamala -harris-path-to-political-heights.

Tolan, Casey. "Why Some of Kamala Harris' Biggest Fans Are in Canada." *San Jose (CA) Mercury News.* Last modified May 8, 2019. https://www.mercurynews.com/2019/05/07/kamala-harris-high -school-montreal-canada-yearbook/.

"Transcript: Kamala Harris' DNC Speech." CNN, August 20, 2020. https:// www.cnn.com/2020/08/19/politics/kamala-harris-speech-transcript /index.html.

Weil, Elizabeth. "Kamala Harris Takes Her Shot." *Atlantic*, May 2019. https://www.theatlantic.com/magazine/archive/2019/05/kamala -harris-2020-campaign/586033/.

LEARN MORE

Biography: Kamala Harris
  https://www.biography.com/political-figure/kamala-harris

Campbell, Janis. *Kamala Harris*. New York: Lucent, 2019.

Harris, Kamala. *The Truths We Hold: An American Journey*. New York: Penguin, 2019.

Kamala D. Harris, US Senator for California
  https://www.harris.senate.gov

Obama White House Archives: Joe Biden
  https://obamawhitehouse.archives.gov/vp

Schwartz, Heather E. *Joe Biden: From Scranton to the White House*. Minneapolis: Lerner Publications, 2021.

INDEX